Moving Ba...

Future

With compliments from Jeremy Farrell, Project Manager

Good day,

I am a project and transformation manager with experience spanning industries, organisations, and technologies.

I compiled this guide during the COVID-19 pandemic lockdown to assist those people assigned to manage their organisation's 're-location' back to the office. There is a possibility they have little project management expertise.

This is my 'offering' to them in managing risk and delivering a suitable working environment.

Please pass it on as you see fit. If I can be of assistance in some way, please drop me a line.

Best regards

Jeremy Farrell

Farrelljp63@gmail.com

Mobile: 0773 5691 522

https://www.jpfarrell.co.uk

CONTENTS

1. Introduction 7

   A Case Study – Noland University 10

2. Enterprise Risk 11

   PESTLE 14

   Noland University 17

3. Strategic Opportunity and Change 22

   Strategy 22

   The StarModel™ 25

4. Managing Project Risk 29

   Defining and Managing your risks 29

   Risk Register 36

5. Managing the Change 45

   The priority of personal health & safety 52

6. 6 Keys to Project health 57

7. Initiating your Re-location project 61

8. Project Startup 63

   Defining Business Benefits 63

   Critical Questions for the 'sponsor' now: 65

   Early draft Business Case example 69

   Why the Business Case is essential for the immediate future. 73

Project Brief / Charter 75

Define the Scope... 76

Define the Project.. 79

Defining the project Deliverable or Product 85

9.   Planning the Re-location... 91

Project Approach 91

Project Management Organisation Structure 94

What   made   the   Office-to-Remote   move straightforward?... 97

What makes the Remote-to-Office move complex?... 99

What don't we know? 101

Scheduling Product Completion 102

Building the project schedule 118

The schedule in a Gantt Chart 120

10.   Manage the Project 123

A note on meetings 125

Tracking the project health 127

Project progress report examples 130

Action Log 133

Issue and Change Register... 135

Managing your costs.. 137

Managing Product quality 141

Planning your project resources – teams, equipment, services, materials 143

Designing and Managing project communications ... 145

11.   Closing the project 147

12.   Conclusion 152

Figure 1 - Example Risk Register for the COVID-19 move 38

Figure 2 - Map Re-location risks with Probability, Impact, and Priority 42

Figure 3 – SOME Risks associated with COVID-19 in office workspaces 52

Figure 4 - 6 Keys Project Health Template 58

Figure 5 - Early draft Business Case 71

Figure 6 - Project Definition example 79

Figure 7 - Project Deliverable / Product example 85

Figure 8 – Further Project 'Approach' examples 92

Figure 9 - An example of a Project Management Team structure 94

Figure 10 - Responsible, Accountable, Consult, Inform with examples 95

Figure 11 - The Office-to-Remote actions are highlighted 98

Figure 12 - Remote-to-Office scope example 100

Figure 13 - Example PBS for a Workplace Re-location .. 105

Figure 14 - WBS Level 3 Example 108

Figure 15 - Example of building a schedule with Level 3 115

Figure 16 - Illustrative Scheduling - Conceptual only 121

Figure 17 - 6 Key Indicators of Project Health 127

Figure 18 - Stakeholder health indicators 128

Figure 19 - Business Benefits Realisation indicators 128

Figure 20 - Work and Schedule indicators 129

Figure 21 - Team performance indicators 129

Figure 22 - Scope health indicators 130

Figure 23 - Risk health indicators 130

Figure 24 - Team Reporting Template 131

Figure 25 - Project Manager Report Template.............. 132

Figure 26 - Action Log Example 134

Figure 27 - Issue / Change Register Example................ 136

Figure 28 - Examples of cost elements in workplace transitions.. 140

1. INTRODUCTION

In February 2020, remote working seemed to be the domain of consultants, sales professionals, and freelancers. By May 2020, a Gallup poll showed that 65% of US respondents had worked from home in the previous two weeks. Compare this to only 25% in September 2019.

Most people who have made the transition from working in the office to remote working did so in a whirlwind of urgency. In the chaos that was the initiation of lockdown, most transitions from the office to home appear successful. In most cases, these were crisis responses enacted without an emergency plan or project manager. Now we must take a more measured approach to the post-lockdown world of work.

Never have we seen this level of uncertainty, nor have the stakes ever been higher. We are looking at a pandemic and lockdowns that have crippled economies. This transition from lockdown to a new way of working is at a pivotal moment in history and a watershed moment for your company. The return is not to the old normal. It is a return to the next normal – a return to the future. And *nobody* knows how the next normal looks. The business case for the application of proven project management techniques is self-evident.

I started writing 'Back to the Future' just as Lockdown in the UK went into the second month. I blogged about 'Lockdown Fatigue' as the domestic and economic reality of COVID-19 was hitting home. As the second month of

Lockdown progressed, I was reading reports regarding the challenges and the opportunities arising from the pandemic and lockdown, and how to mitigate damage or seize the moment for competitive advantage. I heard some leadership talking of a 'lift and shift' return to normal for their employees. If you only shift back to the *old* normal, you are exposing your organisation to many threats and ignoring the opportunities.

Many businesses cannot sustain the work-from-home model for long and that many people will welcome going back. Going to the office lends a routine, a daily rhythm, to get up and leave the house with a destination every day. It draws the line at the end of the day – separating work and home. Consultancy, McKinsey, found in a June 2020 survey that "100 executives at firms across the country and across industries... expect 80 per cent of their workforce, on average, to be back on-site by September and that 88 per cent will be back by December".

Accommodating the interests and preferences of both work-from-office (WFO) and work-from-home (WFH) team members makes for an interesting dynamic.

We are all experiencing distress during the pandemic and associated lockdown. The future is uncertain, and employees insecure. We are talking about the re-location of jobs, roles, and people. Many companies are making such decisions without the input of the employees.

Employees do not want to learn of changes informally. If they hear informally, there are gaps in the story, and they join the dots on their own. They fill the gaps with the prevailing mood. Then speculation and rumour start. To counter this, the messaging must be proactive, planned, crafted, and crystal clear. Trust and confidence call for transparency in leadership. You must tell employees what you know, and don't know. Respect them, and they trust you. When they believe you, they gain confidence and focus on their work. Many employees feel like resources and not valued individuals, and right now, they have a great need to be more than a resource. You have your part to play in changing that perception.

You need staff to be motivated, focused and engaged with their work at this disruptive time. As you pursue your new strategy, you will go through iterations of change. This constant flux is unsettling for team members and poses challenges for leaders and managers. Although many people will think that your Re-location project is about the technical and tangible, the non-technical will be the success factors for your project.

This book is not about moving employee workstations, workplaces, or workspaces. It is about successfully delivering your 2020 plans, amongst changes in company strategy, organisational design, customer relationships, leadership, processes, technology, skills, and jobs. All at the same time.

A Case Study – Noland University

At times I will use the fictitious 'Noland University' as an illustration of points being made. LU is a composite of Higher Education institutions and not representing any specific university. Universities are a useful example of a complex global enterprise faced by a revolution in the marketplace and operating models, as you will see.

Part One of Back to the Future provides a context for your project. The second half of 2020 is very different from the first half. So different in fact, that every project will start with baselines that will almost inevitably have changed by the end.

We start with a look at Enterprise Risk, then consider the pressures on business models to meet the new economy. The re-location of staff post-lockdown is a Tactical project, while strategic changes are being formulated. Therefore, we also look at Project Risk, and the Organisational Change Management required. This positions us for **Part Two**, which tackles the essentials of managing the re-location project of 2020. In Part Two, we consider the project Initiation and Startup, the Planning, Execution and Controlling, and Closure.

The transition to new working arrangements makes for a useful real-world example of the challenges and complexity of moving Back to the Future and provides tips, traps, techniques, and templates for the transition.

2. ENTERPRISE RISK

"The best possible plan today is merely a strawman that will need near-continuous recalibration and change." McKinsey Risk Practice 5/21/2020[1]

Organisations currently operate in the most uncertain of environments. Uncertainty means unpredictability, and that involves risk. Managing risk at the enterprise level includes social, political, commercial, operational, regulatory, competitive, technical, and environmental risk categories. A working definition of Enterprise Risk Management (ERM) is *'the methods and processes used by organisations to manage risks and seize opportunities related to the achievement of their objectives.'* (Wikipedia, June 2020)

September 11, 2001, is etched in the memory of everyone old enough to understand the world-changing impact of that terrorist atrocity. It had a devastating effect on the world's largest economy. We know when that war started. Events of that day initiated a war nearly seven thousand miles away from the attack, in Afghanistan. By 2011 the Afghanistan and Iraq wars had cost the USA more than seven trillion US dollars. Spending on domestic security escalated as we put risk management measures in place.

---

[1]   https://www.mckinsey.com/business-functions/risk/our-insights/return-a-new-muscle-not-just-a-plan

We thought we knew what motivated the attackers, and we thought we knew what the enemy looked like.

The coronavirus scenario is not dissimilar. It originated in a little-known part of the world but has wrought more havoc on the people of the earth than acts of terror and revolution. Coronavirus is a global threat to everything we hold dear. Our global response has been proportional to the danger of the invisible disease. Our response has consequences for the balance of economic power, and undoubtedly political power within and between countries.

We cannot mark the date on which the COVID-19 war started. It crept into the fabric of society, spreading exponentially from a city in China in December 2019. This virus came to the attention of the world in late-January of 2020. The deaths and transmission rates are staggering. The magnitude and velocity and global dispersion of the virus left us reeling. It has exposed fault lines in business and society, which are driving change on a scale and speed never seen before.

Manufacturing, food distribution, and medical supplies were severely disrupted. Social distancing rules have caused many small businesses to close. Millions of people are losing their jobs. Billions of dollars have been redirected from public sector projects or borrowed from the treasury, to support health services. Companies are being kept afloat by government financial assistance. As we come out of the lockdowns, the marketplace has changed in many ways, and our enterprises must redefine and reposition themselves.

Typical commercial objectives for business in 2020 will have included the following elements:

- Increase sales revenue
- Increase services revenue
- Increase in profit
- Increase dividends
- Grow shareholder value
- Innovate
- Eliminate waste
- Optimise supply chains
- Digital transformation
- Mergers and Acquisitions
- Employee engagement, talent attraction and retention

The realities of the marketplace in the second half of 2020 include the following obstacles to the 2020 objectives mentioned above.

- Local and Regional Recession
- Unemployment crisis
- Global depression
- Travel and trade constraints
- Supply Chain vulnerabilities
- Increased input costs
- Increased distribution costs
- Physical distancing
- New employment expectations

Consumer behaviours are changing. Business-to-Business (B2B) and Business-to-Consumer (B2C) business models are under review. Leadership are looking at their strategy, the organisational structure, talent attraction, development and retention, process efficiencies, and technology.

PESTLE

Considering the context above, we can put Enterprise Risks into the following broad categories of the mnemonic 'PESTLE'. This stands for Political, Economic, Social, Technological, Legal, and Environmental types. These are not all contributing to Project Risks but note them for later discussion.

Political Risks are currently visible in discredited national leaders, partisan politics, power-plays, and misdirection. We see blame-shifting, nation-state vs pan-global institutions, and business interests holding sway with politicians. This is going to play out for months and years to come and cause considerable uncertainty for business scenario planners.

Economic and Commercial Risks are self-evident in the poor economic indicators and emerging projections. Unemployment is heading for an all-time high, and economies are anticipating the worst performance since the Great Depression. People without jobs will not have discretionary money to spend. Commercial models must change to meet new consumption patterns.

Technological Risks are in the leapfrog effect of innovations arising from the pandemic. Informal networks of employees have found creative ways to leverage their knowledge for the common good. Organisations can leverage that inventiveness to find new commercial offerings. Many companies found ways to accelerate and scale their offerings to meet the demands of secure, robust remote collaboration.

Regulatory Risks are seen in constraints arising in different industries and over specific products. New controls will be proposed around health, transport, production, and supply. At the same time, some regulations are being changed because they have proven irrelevant or inhibitors for responsible production and consumption. Relaxing rules can lower the historical barriers to entry of new businesses.

Environmental Risks are illustrated by the current impact of COVID-19. There is debate on the source of the coronavirus, whether a wet food market or biological laboratory. The high-risk laboratory had done an environmental risks assessment. This looked at the possibility of contamination from the labs into the environment and the impact on the environment. They would have designed the labs and protocols around risk elimination. The wet market would not. An enterprise in Italy would not have included the possibility of a novel virus in a wet market in Wuhan Province, bringing the Italian economy to a halt.

Social and Cultural Risks are related to economic risks. Still, mental health and social cohesion are also significantly impacted by lockdowns and social media. Unethical business practices or waste will be punished by consumers who can switch loyalties with a click. Social awareness and citizen activism are finding their voices, as seen by recent BLM protests and the consequences for state power structures. Companies must find ways to engage with employees and the community in creating meaningful work and responsible delivery.

#

Noland University

An excellent example of the types of changes that have been forced upon a business comes from higher education - private universities and colleges. Many private schools will recognise themselves in many examples.

It is an extremely competitive landscape, with competition from entrepreneurial degree-issuing 'universities', online education, the university of google, and the economy. The coronavirus and consequences of COVID-19 on universities in the United Kingdom have created the perfect storm.

In November of 2019, the management of Noland set the strategy for 2020 and beyond, called Vision 2020. In November there was no thought of closed borders into the United Kingdom. No theory of a global event preventing foreign students' travel. Vision 2020, therefore, was all growth-oriented which included increasing the number of local and international students as well as filling up spare capacity in the residences. And making more use of the campus buildings to generate income from conferences and summer schools.

The employee climate has been mixed, so vision 2020 was also intended to improve employee engagement. The attraction and retention of top talent into the University management and academic staff is a priority item.

When looking at the future of the next normal when restrictions are lifted in some shape or form, it cannot be guaranteed that the borders will be open again. Even if borders are opened, students must find fees, travel, and living expenses. You cannot just arrive and get a student job, because millions of newly unemployed are vying for any kind of employment.

Vision 2020 has the following business objectives:

- Increase enrolments / revenue
- Increase foreign students / revenue
- Increase residence utilisation / revenue
- Increase conferences and Summer schools/revenue
- Increase research grants
- Increase accessibility
- Reduce maintenance costs
- Develop online offerings
- Engage employees, Reduce attrition

An assessment of Enterprise Risks for Noland would have included the following under the PESTLE headings:

Political risks would have been focused on Brexit negotiations and the impact they would have on freedom of movement for students and academics. Foreign relations would be high on the list, as would government relations and lobbying.

Economic and commercial risks included the attraction of students and academics, occupation rate of residences, government subsidies, and competitive new universities. The strength of overseas students' foreign exchange rate and the stability of their economies are of interest.

Socio-cultural risks included the need to develop a racially diverse and wholly inclusive culture. There is a need to increase access for students from marginalised groups.

Technological risks include constraints on existing skills and infrastructure as the demand for online education increases. New competitors can leapfrog Noland on technology and are ahead in developing online curricula.

Legal or Regulatory risks include the opening up of the HE sector to new degree-issuing universities. At the same time, the barriers to entry for competitors are lowered, other rules are applied that are challenging for an established bureaucratic enterprise to follow.

Environmental risks at Noland were considered in terms of impact on the natural environment, and not of threats to the Noland built environment.

Such is the academic year in the United Kingdom that a lockdown which goes into the second half of 2020 has the following probable impact :

- Reduced First Year enrolments
- Reduced International students
- Reduced residential income
- Reduced conferences and Summer schools
- Reduced travel to the UK for overseas students and staff
- Weakened currency exchange rates for foreign students
- Status quo of research grants
- Status quo of accessibility for students
- The urgency of online development
- Freeze special projects and non-essential hiring
- Employee engagement risk
- New Health and Safety requirements for offices and other workplaces

If an Enterprise Risk Management Plan existed, it couldn't have included many of the actual events arising with the advent of the virus. Now the previously unidentified Risk Events have occurred, there is a critical need for a review of enterprise strategy and tactical responses. COVID-19 has created opportunities and threats which need to be considered.

At the end of March, the majority of staff who could work from home moved to do so. Other staff are on furlough. The university evacuated the residences and created an online education platform. It has been a challenging time of the academic year to be working remotely. The pressure is rising on the 're-location' of staff before the September holiday period.

This is the context for Noland appointing a project manager to 're-locate' the necessary teams, even when the strategy is being revised.

The analysis of Enterprise Risks has heightened the need for an urgent review of enterprise strategies. Clearly, the threats posed by the COVID-19 pandemic and its aftermath could have severe consequences. Conversely, there is always opportunity in adversity. Changes in strategy will frequently drive organisational change, which has a direct bearing on the Re-location project.

3. STRATEGIC OPPORTUNITY AND CHANGE

Strategy

Leaders everywhere are wrestling with the impact of COVID-19. There are operational lessons to be learned, while consumer behaviours have changed. Changes in customer values, disposable income, discernment, and purchasing channels pose a threat to some businesses and opportunities. Your organisation may have to change dramatically or simply adapt offerings and channels. Opportunities may arise for new products and services in new markets. While refining or replacing the business strategy, the organisational structure may need to change. Or the processes may change, or the people, or the technology.

Noland University, for example, needs to explore options in response to specific societal and academic shifts. Some of the choices must result in urgent tactical projects, and others are improving operational systems. Consider the following more apparent challenges and opportunities for Higher Education:

- How much of the 'business' of educating can remain as distance learning?
- How much of the service can only be provided on-campus?
- How might on-campus and distance education be blended?

- How do we compete with new and agile online universities?
- How do we manage expectations of the reduced cost of online education?
- How do we optimise the use of buildings on campus?
- How do we increase non-educational income to supplement fees and reduced residence rentals?
- How much of our administration can become remote work?
- How do we leverage remote working to reduce costs but increase efficiencies and reduce unwanted attrition?
- What must happen RIGHT NOW to maintain business continuity?

Transformation through crisis

Throughout the crisis, we have seen employees innovate in solutions for their company and community. The most obvious of these are the innovations regarding ventilators, treatments, vaccines, and 'field hospitals'. Some occurred at speed because processes were streamlined, or more resources assigned to legacy bottlenecks in administration. There are examples of innovation and implementation in many countries, and cases of gross failure to do so.

The organisations that survive and thrive are those that choose to learn the lessons, good and bad, from their experience. Not only do they learn, but they dare to make decisions, act on the opportunities and manage the threats. Implementation could require organisational changes that affect your projects.

Here is an example of questions your leadership may be asking themselves. This list is not exhaustive by any means!

- Strategy
  - What did we do in the war against COVID-19?
  - What lessons have we learned about our capabilities?
  - What is our meaningful destination?
  - Are we rethinking our industry's doctrines?
  - What futures do we want to build?
  - What new industry and consumer patterns are we noticing?
  - What is our strategy if coronavirus comes back every year?
  - What buffers have we created to reduce the impact of disruption?
  - Which other disruptions are we ignoring?
- Structure
  - How is our organisation adapting to the next normal?
  - What have we learnt from Coronavirus that will help us prepare for other disruptive forces?
  - What is our organisation doing to build back better?
  - Is our model adaptive and resilient?
- Processes
  - How are we deploying breakthrough technologies to solve big problems?
  - Are our innovations finding new ground?
  - What 'wisdom' demands challenging?

- People
  - o Do we have transformational and adaptive leaders?
  - o How will our organisation ensure our peoples' wellbeing?
  - o What talent do we need to attract?
  - o What capabilities must we develop?
  - o What is our approach to remote and flexible working?

The StarModel™

Jay Galbraith, Organisational Design consultant, created the StarModel™, which helps categorise aspects of the business impacted by changes in strategy. These areas may impact your Re-locate project. These five factors interact to provide a framework for organisational design:

- Strategy
- Structure
- People
- Rewards
- Process (Technology)

Structure

Change in strategy will affect some teams more than others, and some jobs will change or be lost. You need to be aware of plans to change the structure.

- If a centralised organisation becomes federalised, does it change where teams will be based, or the size of the team?

- If a centrally based head office splits into regional or geographic areas, what is the requirement?
- If a regional organisation is to be centralised because you can perform local operations with remote workers, what is the impact on your project?
- Do you need to include this in your communications/change strategy?

Processes (and Technology)

One realisation is that we do not need all of our processes as they currently are. When those get reviewed, the company may be able to automate some of the job functions due to simplified procedures.

- Tasks may move to other departments, which could affect staffing and seating of the sending and receiving teams.
- Efficient use of systems eliminates some tasks previously required for audit.
- Physical and technical security requirements may change.
- Teams may need new processes.

People

Changes in organisational structure, job design, processes, and technologies will impact on employees and teams. It could bring about fundamental changes in what people do from day-to-day, and it could result in restructuring and loss of jobs. The stress and trauma must be top of mind during consultation and planning if you want this to succeed tactically and strategically.

As mentioned often, your employees and teams must be engaged, enabled, empowered, and encouraged to embrace the changes. Neglecting them is the biggest mistake we can make. They must be aware, motivated, educated, and capable for this transition or transformation to succeed.

Project Risks

If you were the project manager of the Re-location at Noland, what would you be worried about? What are the primary threats to the successful delivery of your project outcome?

Next, we will explore the Project Risks of a Tactical Re-location during the organisational changes that can affect who does what, where, when, and how.

4. MANAGING PROJECT RISK

Your project sponsor may only be thinking of the logistics of a Re-location. As you have seen, complexity and risk abound. Logistics are only one part of the project as it exists alongside many projects. As the Project Manager, your knowledge of your company's enterprise-level risks, strategic planning, and organisational changes, empowers you in the determination and management of Project-level Risks. At a project level, you may not be concerned with Political risks. Still, broader insight into Social, Environmental, Technical and Regulatory factors will be valuable.

Your project is Tactical. It has been chosen as immediately necessary for resumption and continuity of the business, even though the corporate strategy is not firmed up. The company is taking the view that it is better to initiate movement in the right direction while they determine the best option. They accept that they could change the scope and requirement while your project is in full flight.

As we have discussed, a change in strategy could change the organisational structure, roles, responsibilities, locations, processes and technology.

Defining and Managing your risks

Given that your primary project objective is the return of the necessary workforce to a safe workplace, your principal project risks relate to completing the environment in which people will work. I previously said it will be intangibles which will determine the success of the project. Those intangibles are employee perception of safety, and their willingness to return to the workplace. If you get that wrong, you have failed. You will only get that right with rigorous project management and, considering the prevalence of coronavirus, this highlights diligent Risk Management.

As PM, you must deliver to Scope, Cost, and Time, but ultimately you are judged by Product Quality. The quality of your product – a safe and healthy workplace – is paramount. If the resulting environment is unsafe for employees, you score no points for Scope, Cost and Time.

Let's consider the facets of a COVID-19 safe working environment.

We will look at Product Breakdown Structures later on. Still, the following are Products within workstreams of the project that need to be correctly in place before all staff feel you have met your duty of care.

1. Air purification must meet any government or union-specified standard.
2. Building and office access should be controlled and low-touch readers and doors.
3. Desks must be suitably spaced with appropriate screening where needed or requested.
4. Sanitisation protocols must be in place and managed with clear accountability. (I would put Service Level Agreements in place with cleaning services.)
5. Parking bays must allow for appropriate distancing when accessing a car.
6. Common areas should be demarcated with 'safe zones' even if government guidance does not require it.
7. Ablutions should be allocated to particular employee groups to increase a sense of 'ownership'.
8. PPE should be available to staff on request.
9. Arrival and departure schedules should be documented, agreed, and enforced.
10. The system should not put employees in the uncomfortable position of challenging their colleagues on bad practice.
11. A third-party should be responsible for the 'application' (i.e. enforcement)of the policies.

The Quality standards for these project products must be clearly defined and each workstream held accountable for adherence. (These are illustrative and therefore not necessarily a comprehensive list.)

In their guidance on 'Working safely during the coronavirus outbreak – a short guide', the UK Health and Safety Executive say to ask the following questions:

"Who should go to work? You should think about:

- *where and how your work is carried out, consider if there are jobs and tasks that can be changed to reduce risk.*
- *Identifying everyone in your business who can work from home – if they can, they should.*
- *Providing (the) equipment needed for employees to work safely and effectively at home (for example, laptops, mobile phones, video conferencing equipment).*
- *Keeping in regular contact with people working from home, making sure you discuss their wellbeing and helping them to feel they are still part of the workforce.*
- *Where it is not possible to work from home, the guidance on social distancing and hygiene (handwashing with soap and water often, for at least 20 seconds) should be followed.*
- *The minimum number of people needed to carry out work tasks safely."*

https://www.hse.gov.uk/news/assets/docs/working-safely-guide.pdf accessed 31 May 2020.

The determination of who should work at home, and who should work at the office is probably not your responsibility. This should be determined by the business in conjunction with HR, Health & Safety, unions and employees. If it is put on your plate, it is the first activity and critical success factor in the project. Since you will be held accountable for implementing the scope of the project, you need to know how the population is determined. This determination of departments, teams, and individuals to move is a critical variable that will probably change during the project.

Wherever possible anyone who can do their job from home with minor adjustment to their environment or tasks, should be encouraged to work from home. There is too much at stake here. We cannot pull people back to a higher risk workplace without due consideration.

I have a word of caution from the beginning of the book quoting a McKinsey survey in June 2020. There has been a lot of talk about how we will all be working from home in future. This is not borne out by the surveys of chief executives. I believe that by the end of the year, about eighty per cent of office-based staff will be returning to the office.

Project Risk categories will vary by organisation. Risk categories or sources that can affect the Re-location could be:

- A resurgence of COVID-19.
- Weak or shifting requirements.
- Change Control.
- Procurement.
- Project Management and Team.
- Construction.
- Equipment.
- Facilities.
- Service providers.
- Employee relations.
- Regulations.
- Policies and Procedures.
- Processes.
- Technology.
- Stakeholder Management.
- Communications and Change Management.

Risk management is both art and science. It draws on our personal experience, lessons learned, templates, methods, and best practice in the industry or field of the project. Risks abound in any new initiative, mainly when producing something unique. It means we are breaking new ground and have to scan the horizon and environment for events that might impact the performance or completion of the project.

Other factors that increase the risk profile of your project are:

- Any new systems for staff?
- The number of staff being moved?
- Is any of the infrastructure a new technology? (eg. Air purification; Access control)
- Are the installers familiar with the technology?
- How many suppliers are involved?
- Are the dependencies clear?
- What is the lead time on equipment?
- How many workstreams are there?
- What condition is the target workspace in?
- The number of people with an opinion on what you are doing!

The importance and context of the project may raise the concern of a risk in one project but lower it in another. People need to understand that raising risk is not saying that event is *going* to happen, but it is *possible under certain conditions*.

Let's use the Relo as an example of risk identification and classification with a possible response:

There is another office location which is not in the scope of your project, but you feel there is a chance it might be brought in scope before you finish. You raised this as a risk. Based on your knowledge of the organisation, you feel there is a low probability that it will happen, but a high impact if it does. You have raised it because of the possibility. You consider the impact and whether you need to take any formal action to have it specified as out of scope. At very least to agree with your Sponsor on how to deal with such a request. For example, you might agree with the Sponsor to write a clause in the new lease agreement that gives you the first option on the empty Floor above your offices. Because it is a low probability, you might not spend much time and energy developing a risk mitigation plan for this specific risk.

There is another risk on your project related to project cost management and project procurement management. The risk is if there is more than a thirty-day delay signing a contract for goods and services, the price will increase by 10%. You have spoken to procurement, and they are negotiating as a priority. Still, you must ask your Sponsor to put some money aside to cover that 10% increase if it comes to pass.

Risks are based on uncertain events and assumptions, around which you will make decisions on how to mitigate or eliminate probability. I call an assumption an unqualified risk. You are making decisions based on something that may or may not be true but could probably be confirmed now so that your choices are fact-based.

There are risks that you can anticipate, and then there are those which are so improbable but catastrophic an impact that you do not even think about them. We find ourselves in just such a position with the COVID-19 pandemic.

Risk Register

The project risks you identify must go into a register as part of your Risk Management Plan.

The Risk Register can be a standalone document, or, as I prefer, a worksheet in an Excel workbook. The columns you have, or where you locate them is a matter of preference. However, you must track dates, progress, Probability, Impact, Priority/Severity and status updates. Actions for Risk Management should be created in the Action Log for execution. Having the Action Log and the Risk Register in the same document is why I like using Excel.

As discussed earlier, it is the employees' acceptance of the environment and the Re-location at the office that will determine the success of your project. In the next chapter, we will discuss organisational change management.

Figure 1 - Example Risk Register for the COVID-19 move

Risk ID	Xref	Risk short description	Risk Long description	Management action
1	A26	Infection - Office equipment	Infection from office equipment such as printers, scanners, kitchens, vending machines.	Sanitising gel and wipes at the place of use.
2	A27	Infection - Desks	Infection from shared desks, materials placed on the counter, molecules from a passer-by.	Review frequency of disinfection.
3	A23	Infection - Access points	Infection from biometric readers, handles, push plates.	Install touchless security, automated doors, sanitiser and wipes at point of entry.

Risk ID	Xref	Risk short description	Risk Long description	Management action
4	A30	Infection - Proximity of workstations	Infection from respiratory transmission	Spacing and perspective of workstations, screens.
5	C04	Infection - Ablutions	Infection from poor hygiene in the use of toilets, taps, basins, exit handles	Put access control on doors, review frequency of cleaning, sanitiser at points of entry. Push doors open from inside.
6	A22	Infection - From visitors	Infection from people visiting the workspace for any purpose.	Restrict visitor access, create 'safe spaces' for visitor interaction.
7		Infection - Incoming packaging, Documents	Contamination from packaging, contents, documents, clothing, trolleys etc	Provide some kind of spray or device with disinfectant properties that will

Risk ID	Xref	Risk short description	Risk Long description	Management action
				not damage the packaging or contents.
8		Infection - Social distancing in walkways	Infection from inadequate pedestrian space or poor compliance.	Create one-way passages with some room for passing, but only one-way.
9		Infection - Vulnerable people	Infection of vulnerable members of your team or team members going home to vulnerable people.	To be reviewed by needs.
10		Infection - Meeting rooms	Infection from the use of meeting rooms and other common facilities.	Sanitising gel and wipes at the place of use, and cleaning frequency

Risk ID	Xref	Risk short description	Risk Long description	Management action
				increased. Provide technology that does not need direct contact with whiteboards or pens (and/or make the pens single-use disposable).

Figure 2 - Map Re-location risks with Probability, Impact, and Priority

Remote-to-Office Risks	Type	P	I	S	Actions
Contract delay for a new lease	Procurement	Nil	Nil	Nil	Not applicable for RTU
New offices not vacant on time	Facilities	L	L	L	Depends on decisions re remote work. Staff can continue working remotely.
External Fibre connection not complete	Facilities	L	L	L	Depends on decisions re remote work. Staff can continue working remotely.

Remote-to-Office Risks	Type	P	I	S	Actions
Internal cabling not ready for our networking	Facilities	Nil	Nil	Nil	Ignore for RTU
Furniture not delivered on time .	Procurement	L	L	L	Depends on decisions re remote work. Staff can continue working remotely.
Onward chain delays	Legal	Nil	Nil	Nil	Ignore for RTU
Secure access not complete	Facilities	Nil	Nil	Nil	Ignore for RTU
COVID-19 readiness not signed off	HR	M	M	M	Staff continue to work remotely until signed.

Remote-to-Office Risks	Type	P	I	S	Actions
Resignations of staff who cannot move	HR	Nil	Nil	Nil	Ignore for RTU
Labour court re the move	HR	Nil	Nil	Nil	Ignore for RTU
Accessibility not available on time	HR	Nil	Nil	Nil	Ignore for RTU
Servers not available	IT	Nil	Nil	Nil	Ignore for RTU
WiFi not accessible	IT	Nil	Nil	Nil	Ignore for RTU

5. MANAGING THE CHANGE

The coronavirus pandemic can accelerate organisational transformation. Your project can be an enabler as a change agent and creating the new 'workplace'.

In the words of doctors, nurses, economists, politicians, bankers, and business leaders, 'we have never seen anything like this before'. The changes driven by the coronavirus lockdowns across the world are unprecedented in their downstream impact. Most models of organizational change anticipate proactively planning change strategies and projects. Even with the best consultants and commitment of management, we know as many as 70% of corporate transformation projects fail*. Although we have learned a lot in the years since that figure was published, we also have a legacy of entrenched thinking. Thousands of small to medium-sized businesses have no concept of managed change. They will be facing the unknown with only the tools they have always used.

The established organizational change models could not have envisaged the magnitude of the change that would be thrust upon organisations of every size in an exceptionally short time. One of the better-known models of organizational transformation is that of John Kotter. His eight-stage model starts with establishing a sense of urgency, then creating a guiding coalition, and then developing a vision and strategy. He proceeds with the fourth stage - the communication of the change vision. Next is empowering broad-based action then generating short-term wins, consolidating gains and producing more change. Finally, anchoring new approaches in the culture.

1. Establish a sense of urgency.
2. Create a guiding coalition.
3. Develop a vision and strategy.
4. Communicate the change vision.
5. Empower people to broad-based action.
6. Generate short-term wins.
7. Consolidate gains and produce more change.
8. Anchor new approaches in the culture.

In the current business environment, there is no shortage of a sense of urgency, a compelling reason to act, to implement change. Not only to handle the immediate impact of the virus but also for recovery and sustainability after that.

The first COVID move to everyone being remote was relatively easy.

1. One person did an inventory of who had what equipment and access to work from home.
2. Each person moved and configured their home environment.
3. Work carried on with a few small bumps as they learned the new way of working.

The magnitude and velocity of the change to remote ways of working allowed little time for preparation. It was a reactive process using whatever means were at hand for mobilising the organisation's resources to effect the necessary changes. Most organisations had about two weeks of real warning before Lockdown. Awareness of the imperative of change was generated mainly by government and media. Your organisation could lag a little in your messaging. Mass-media created desire or motivation, but not specific to your organisation.

In stark contrast, moving 'back' – Re-locating - poses fresh challenges. Guidance, regulations and duty of care obligations complicate the move back. Investors, owners, staff, unions and communities are scanning the economic landscape for signs of hope. Business confidence is low. Consumer confidence is low.

The novelty and energy of moving to remote working mid-March 2020 is wearing thin for many people. They are anxious about their work-life in the coming months and years. They hear about the New Normal, and the Next Normal, but they are not hearing enough from their leaders. The media shaped the messaging around the first move, and employees were filling in the gaps themselves. Employers need to control the messaging now.

Despite the hardship, people have shown resilience in past crises, and economies have recovered. We know we can overcome the challenges that lie ahead. Staff want to feel part of the future. They need to be secure in their jobs. If your message is unclear, employees can misinterpret decisions on who moves back to the office and who stays remote.

The Gallup organisation tells us that resilient employees and teams have the following attributes:

- They know what is expected of them.
- They have the right tools to do their job.
- They regularly have the opportunity to do what they do best.
- They find their work meaningful.
- They believe their co-workers are as committed to quality as they are.

Consider the impact on employee resilience if your colleagues feel ignored, disrespected, in the transformation decisions. The climate is going to suffer, the employees wondering if they matter to the company at a human level. The burden of responsibility sits with management before, during, and after the pandemic is under control. I understand that their companies do not know what is next. Still, they need to share all the information that they do have with their employees.

Creating interest and overcoming resistance to change requires creative and clear communication strategies. In planning the Re-location, the project manager must put together a communications plan that incorporates each stakeholder and stakeholder group. This integrated plan includes management, shareholders, employees, customers, and the community. You will draw on the expertise of corporate communications, marketing, human resources, and labour relations, crafting the communications strategy.

Do not underestimate the impact on your managers in navigating this change and the new skills they must learn. Leading a hybrid on/off-site team can be more complicated than entirely offsite. I use a simple model a manager can use as he maintains momentum while the Re-location is happening. It is also a simple 'checklist' they can use going forwards. This model is necessary for motivating your team and individuals:

1. **Engage** in clarifying expectations, coach for improvement, connect for relationship and meaning.
2. **Enable** employees with the knowledge, education, and equipment they need to perform.
3. **Encourage** – 'give courage' – in performing the tasks, showing trust, consulting, and requiring excellence.
4. **Evaluate** performance by outcomes and not input/effort, nor output. Monitor regularly and provide timely feedback. Evaluation and Engagement are overlapping in the model.

In an integrated communication strategy, you will have a balance of approaches that indicate control and commitment from the top but provide the feeling of ownership on the ground. It is people who inhibit change for various personal reasons. You are seeking to win over the resistance of inhibitors and build motivation for change.

A simple model you can apply to your organisational change is the ADKAR™ model of the Prosci Institute. They created the five steps which help frame the essentials of a successful transition. The steps are:

1. Awareness
2. Desire
3. Knowledge
4. Ability
5. Reinforcement

In ADKAR, you create Awareness of the change, create the Desire or motivation to participate in the change constructively. You evaluate the Knowledge that is required to deliver on the change and be sure that the employees have the Ability to translate the Knowledge into practice. The final step of the model is the Reinforcement of the change.

There is a need to personalise the Awareness message. Reinforce why the status-quo is still good for the individual and the company, at the same time as flagging the changes afoot. It is urgent to lead with new empathy and clarity. Remove as much uncertainty as you can, and thereby create the desire to continue to give of our best. Engaging to raise awareness and hope is a crucial aspect of reinforcement at this stage, so that staff feel secure during more change.

You are embarking on more unsettling change for many employees. Engage with them around their concerns and issues. Develop a communications and marketing strategy as part of the change management process. Enable and Empower them with information. Encourage them through the change, and then Evaluate acceptance as the project progresses.

Your change and communication strategy must:

1. Raise Awareness of what is happening and why it is essential. Share the challenges and opportunities the 'new normal' could present the company with.
2. Create the Desire to be part of the journey by individualising the message. What is in it for each employee? Why you? How will it affect you? What do you think?
3. Determine the education and skills required for the roles and people involved. Make sure the appropriate Knowledge is imparted.
4. Ensure the individual has the Ability to apply the knowledge effectively in their new job.
5. Reinforce the message with regular progress updates, celebrate success, and acknowledge change champions.

The priority of personal health & safety

The priority in the Re-location project is the protection of employee wellbeing when they return to the workplace. Highlighted below are immediate health risks and *some* of the management actions you might propose as part of the move. Your organisation will determine the steps. You will need to complete the steps before the staff are entirely confident about the move.

Five assurances your staff want from you:

- You have complied with government guidance.
- You have performed a risk assessment and shared it with all employees.
- You have taken reasonable steps to enable people to work from home.
- You have taken all reasonable steps to create a working environment with a safe distance between workers.
- You have done everything practical to manage transmission risk if you cannot provide the required distance

Figure 3 – SOME Risks associated with COVID-19 in office workspaces

Risk description	Management action
Infection from office equipment such as printers, scanners, kitchens, vending machines.	Provide sanitising gel and wipes at the place of use.

Infection from shared desks, materials placed on a pedestal, molecules from a passer-by.	Review the frequency of disinfection.
Infection from biometric readers, handles, push plates.	Install touchless security, automated doors, sanitiser and wipes at point of entry.
Infection from respiratory transmission	Correct the spacing and perspective of workstations, screens.
Infection from poor hygiene in the use of toilets, taps, basins, exit handles	Put access control on doors, review frequency of cleaning, sanitiser at points of entry. Push doors open from inside.
Infection from people visiting the workspace for any purpose.	Restrict the access of visitors, create 'safe spaces' for visitor interaction.
Infection from packaging, contents, documents, clothing, trolleys etc	Provide some kind of spray or device with disinfectant properties that will not damage the packaging or contents.

Infection from inadequate pedestrian space or poor compliance.	Create one-way passages with some room for passing, but only one-way.
Infection of vulnerable members of your team or team members going home to vulnerable people.	To be reviewed by needs.
Infection from the use of meeting rooms and other common facilities.	Provide sanitising gel and wipes at the place of use, and increase cleaning frequency. Provide technology that does not need direct contact with whiteboards or pens (and/or make the pens single-use disposable).

In Part Two of Back to the Future, we look at core elements of project management, you must apply in pursuit of successful Re-location.

PART TWO

MANAGING THE PROJECT

6. 6 KEYS TO PROJECT HEALTH

Let's start Part Two, Managing the Project, discussing the Health of Project Relo.

We are into the second half of 2020, and you have been assigned one of the company's most important projects. It makes sense to START with a health check, and instead of spinning our wheels, figuring out how to take the project pulse, we can use 6 Keys to create a simple RAG table.

There are six key indicators you can consider as below. This is a dashboard useful for communicating to all stakeholders, including an excellent early slide in a presentation to SteerCo.

Complete this immediately, even if you only have a rough idea of the answers. Add open questions to the RAIDAR. Review this with your Project Sponsor – get those answers clarified and confirmed. Later sections guide you in determining the actual Red – Amber – Green (RAG) health of the 6 Health indicators.

Figure 4 - 6 Keys Project Health Template

6 Keys	RAG	Comments
Stakeholder Commitment	Green	If you know the main stakeholders, their interest, and how committed they are.
Scope Management	Green	If you understand the scope clearly and see that the Sponsor will be strict about managing it.
Business Benefits	Green	If you understand what business benefits the company expects (if you have the Business Case already).
Risk Management	Green	If you have been given a view of the risks so far and they appear under management control.
Team Performance	Green	If you know who is already involved and how their responsibilities are being executed.
Work and Schedule	Green	If you know the expected work completion at this point and if the future deadlines seem realistic.

Green:	There are no Issues or Exceptions.
Amber:	There are Issues. However, there is an agreed and realistic plan to address them.
Red	There are Issues. However, there is NO current plan or identified solution. Escalation required.

7. INITIATING YOUR RE-LOCATION PROJECT

The project management sections of the book are the phases of the 'Relo' project. The first three phases, the Startup, Initiation and Planning, are not to be bypassed. You will see how essential initial requirements and planning are to the success of your project. We know that most project failures result from poorly defined requirements. Without precise requirements from the sponsor, you are planning with incomplete intelligence. This means you are introducing much risk before you even start with risk management. You are probably making too many planning assumptions. Assumptions are attempts to fill gaps in our knowledge, also show movement, so that our planning carries on. This is false progress. The odds are high that incorrect assumptions will become inconvenient truths.

Startup
The project manager and sponsor clarify the business case, goals and objectives, scope, deliverable, stakeholders. They create the project charter as authorisation to initiate the project.

Initiation
The project manager compiles the management system and expands on the charter to create a project definition and project management plan. We use this for communication and identification of the resources required for the Planning phase.

Planning

The project manager works with subject matter experts to draw on lessons learned, documentation and expertise to identify the activities, dependencies, effort, resources and risks. The project manager enhances the Project Management Plan and compiles a project schedule with durations, costs, dependencies, and resources.

Executing & Controlling

The project manager manages the allocation of work and monitors progress against the plan. She has a project-level perspective of risks, issues, changes, dependencies, and key open actions. Depending on the size of the project, the project manager may fulfil several roles other than the primary one of integration management.

Closing

Exactly as it says, this is the project manager's validation that everything that should be complete is. The project manager asks for executive confirmation and then closes off all of the resource agreements. She hands over the project product or products to the teams that will own them going forwards.

8. PROJECT STARTUP

By the time you open this book, you may well be into the development of the project plan.   However, let me mention the building blocks for getting there.

Defining Business Benefits

Start immediately with the Business Case.

All future evaluation of the project health will validate the progress to produce the benefits anticipated at the beginning. You have been given the project because the move needs to happen. Still, you do not know the criteria used to decide on the solution. Therefore, you do not know the standards by which the progress and outcome will be measured. Is this part of a New Normal programme of change, or does the owner think it can stand alone without being aligned to a goal?

In a perfect world, your 'sponsor' should have the answers to these questions.   Amidst the pandemic, she does not. But you have to push as reasonably as you can to get answers (without ruining the relationship :-)).

The Sponsor should provide a Business Case which details the following:

- Specify how the benefits will be achieved. This is complex because unless it is a total Re-location back to the office, you will need to innovate on the management and communications system. It was less effort when everyone was remote.

- The Critical Success Factors (CSF).
- What procurement sourcing decisions have already been made.
- Who is the Budget holder, and what is the source of project funding?
- The primary business, financial and reputational risks if this fails.

The Business Case should be reviewed at milestones or stage gates to ensure that it is still valid even though the operating environment is in constant flux. The Business Case will grow in detail to a point during initiation and definition, but then be baselined.

Critical Questions for the 'sponsor' now:

Goal

Be Specific:

- What are the business benefits required for the project?
- What are the critical success factors (CSF)?
- What are the priorities outputs for you?
- What is the scope in teams, departments, business units, buildings, locations?

Agree on Metrics:

- How do you want to measure financial progress?
- How do you want to measure work product progress?
- How do we evaluate the business benefits as we progress?

Align with the organisation:

- Where does this project align with strategy?
- What are other projects dependent on this one?
- What projects am I dependent on?

A lack of precise requirements is the number one reason for project failure. If you do not know the Sponsor's goal, you cannot develop an overall plan for achieving it. Without a plan, you are adrift. If you do not know the requirements, you do not see the scope. If you do not see the scope, you do not know the work. If you do not see the work, you cannot break it down to activities with durations and resources you need. If you do not know the work that has to be performed, you will find it challenging to identify what could get in the way of success.

You must know who has to do what, where, when and how. Many of the people performing project tasks will consistently deliver excellence if they know 'Why' their task is essential. This list will include activities intended to minimise risk, overcome cultural obstacles, to improve climate, and increasing levels of employee engagement.

Reality questions
Financials

- What is the budget?
- When are the funds released?

Work and Schedule

- What work has started?
- What is the status of the dependent projects?

Team

- Who has been involved to-date?
- Who had the responsibility before, and where are they?

Risks

- What are the known obstacles, risks, and issues?
- What are the main business Risks if this fails?
- How are the business risks being managed?
- What are the main Constraints on the project?

- What are the main Assumptions behind the chosen direction?

Stakeholders

- Who are the main stakeholders?
- What parts of the organisation are in and out of scope?

Understanding the Options

What is the compelling reason to transition back NOW and not later, when there could be greater certainty? Unpredictable changes in policy or resurgence of the virus could create rework or increase other expenses. Knowing this enables the PM to head-off objections and resistance, and make judgement calls, during the project. If you do not understand why this solution was chosen, you might end up questioning it later, or too late.

- What were alternative approaches considered?
- Why was this solution chosen?
- What criteria were used to delimit the scope?
- If a phased/staged project, how were the priorities determined?
- How open are you to alternatives if they arise during project initiation/definition?
- The benefits of the mix of on-site vs remote (if not a total move) should be clearly identified and justified.

Ensure that ANY open Assumptions are listed as Risks and added to the Action Log for you or your Sponsor to follow up.

Early draft Business Case example

As the PM, you need a clear statement of the reason behind this choice of project. This is the early iteration of the Business Benefits, Scope, Budget, Duration, Risks, Dependencies, and significant work packages.

The need to relocate at least some employees is self-evident, the Business Case is not as straightforward. The Business Case justifies and motivates for the company to spend money or time on transitioning some employees back to the office. Time equals money because of 'opportunity cost'. Assigning labour to a project means not assigning it to another project; therefore, the Re-location must make long-term business sense.

There are several ways of approaching the Re-location of employees with different levels of cost impact. When you take over the project, you will receive the business case as it stands. It is incumbent on you to make sure the benefits expected are realistic. Has the executive chosen the most effective solution, given the variables?

Think about some of the options and their implications.

Do nothing. This is not a terrible option considering we have survived the heart of the crisis working from home. It is the lowest cost, even if we have to upgrade the remote workers' home workplace a little. It has implications for meeting customer expectations in some instances. Some customers will be back at the office and expect their suppliers to do the same. They miss being able to phone us without worrying about family in the background. The option of doing nothing leaves you flexibility and buys you time to make the best possible decision on who to move, where, when, and how.

Do the minimum. Often called 'Minimum Viable Product' (MVP), the aim is to realise the optimal business benefits in the shortest time and least cost. Do you move as many people as you can while meeting all social distancing requirements? Do you bring half a team back to occupy the space previously occupied by the whole team? Do you rotate the half-team every few days or alternate weeks to balance the pros and cons to the staff? Do you bring some departments and not others, so you use double space for one department? This mitigates the risk and limits the costs, but the costs are probably higher than doing nothing.

Do the most. This is probably the highest cost because you are trying to accommodate as many people as possible into existing space or having to lease more space. In uncertain times you probably don't want to be signing leases for more space. Doing 'the most' might actually mean 'doing the most with the least'. That doesn't sound like good news.

Figure 5 - Early draft Business Case

Executive Summary	This is a summary of the sections that follow. Think of it as a single ppt slide with a bulleted list.
Compelling Reason to Act	Why Now? It is not only because Lockdown is lifting. Post-COVID-19 is a different business environment which you need to build in flexibility and responsiveness in the staffing model – NOW!
Business Options	Briefly list the Options considered and why this one was preferred. They may all have been good, so why is this your Project solution? Do not go into details on the non-selected options.
Benefits	o Reduced operating costs? o Flexible workspace? o Compliance with COVID-19 regulations? o An Engaged Workforce? o Attractive to Talent?
Timescale	Are there critical delivery dates? How long do they expect the project to take? Where did they estimate that?
Costs	These are high-level costs unless they already have a detailed project

	schedule with resourcing. It includes labour, construction, materials, furniture, services and so on.
Major Risks	The immediate and short-term risks to the project at the time of drawing up the Business Case. They will be added to and updated as the project progresses. Examples: o If government guidance becomes legally enforceable, costs of return might be higher than planned. o If there is a second wave of coronavirus and everyone has to work from home again, you have already incurred the costs of the initial move. o If the majority of staff want to continue at home, but you need them at the office – what do you do? And is this different if you are unionised?

Why the Business Case is essential for the immediate future.

"Time is of the essence. None of us has seen anything like this in our lifetimes. Our response as business leaders, therefore, should be preparing for something that we have not experienced before." McKinsey Martin Hirt, a senior partner and a global co-leader of McKinsey's Strategy and Corporate Finance practice. [2]

This Re-location is a complex project with implications for the business, employees, and customers if it is not successful. The most crucial task is to clarify the requirements of the Relo project. You must know what outcome is required. You want to ask questions to eliminate assumptions, ambiguities, and uncertainties which can undermine all the other planning activities.

We are all dealing with massive uncertainty; therefore, it is vital that you 'Know What You Know', and 'Know What You Don't Know'. The first are elements of the business that are most predictable or controllable; the second are those which are Assumptions and known Risks. (Assumptions are Risks, but more on that later.)

Asking questions raises your awareness and prompts thought for your Sponsor. Your questions may be the difference between success and failure. It only takes one

---

[2] https://tinyurl.com/yakr6y9n

enquiry that the Sponsor cannot answer to identify more Assumptions/Risks.

Project Brief / Charter

The Project Brief / Charter is your mandate to commit resources to the project. It will contain many of the following aspects, depending on the project environment and needs.

- **Project purpose**. Why are we doing this project?
- **Project objectives**. What are we aiming to produce?
- **High-level requirements**. What are the factors and features to achieve the objectives?
- **Project description** including scope, time and cost constraints.
- **Project risk profile**. What does the organisation see in terms of business, reputation, environmental and regulatory risk areas?
- **Milestones and associated deliverables** (aka Products and Stages) where known.
- **Budget.** What has been allocated to the project and how it is intended to be used?
- **Stakeholders**. Who are the key stakeholders inside and outside of the organisation?
- **Deliverable approval processes**. Who has to review, amend and sign-off the deliverable?
- **Completion criteria**. What is required for final project closure?
- **Project Management Team**. Who is the project manager, and who else makes the top level of the project management team?

Define the Scope

Continual validation and control of the project scope are essential on projects. You need to have a robust Scope Management Plan. The frequency of reviewing the scope will vary on the type and/or the stage of the project. Changes to the Scope could impact on the duration, cost, complexity, risk, dependencies……. the list is long.

The below table lists some of the vital Scope elements you may have asked in a full Office-to-Office move. Broadly speaking, you are wanting to determine:

- o The staff in and out of the scope of the move.
- o The functions, departments, services in and out of the scope of the move.
- o What other locations are in the scope of the move?

Below is an example of the scope for the Relo:

Scope element	Response
Combining existing offices	The configuration of office locations, office requirements, and how many people will continue to work from home full time are unknown.
Departments to move	**In**: All department members who can feasibly and willingly work at the office are in scope.

	Out: People who are working from home effectively and choose to stay as such.
Total number of employees	Approximately 25 of 30 employees.
Staff Facilities	**In**: Normal staff facilities at the office.
	In: Remote staff must be fully equipped to do their jobs and meet OHS requirements.
	In: IT Security requirements must be met for remote workers.
	Out: No printers, desks, cupboards to move.

Define the Project

The answers to the above questions are used to populate a Project Charter and be your mandate to commit resources to rapidly develop a project management plan. If you start the project planning without a sufficiently precise definition, your risk starts high. You already have many critical unknowns. Without clarity, you will be planning with a list of assumptions and heightened risk to your reputation and the organisation success.

You can use a framework like a table below, which I have populated with some examples of answers.

Figure 6 - Project Definition example

Background	<ul><li>'The majority of the workforce is currently working remotely or on furlough due to COVID-19 Lockdown requirements.</li><li>The transition to remote working was done at pace, driven at a team level with some central support. The transition back to 'the next normal' must be centrally coordinated.</li><li>Many staff who have not been able to continue to work from home for various reasons have returned to the office in line with the easing</li></ul>

	of restrictions. They are observing social /physical distancing rules where possible. ○ We do not have a policy on physical distancing at the office, waiting on the government. We must start anyway. ○ We do not know if there will be redundancies, but some are likely in the ABC Department. ○ We have to return to optimal operations as soon as possible as some functions have not performed at the same standard as before Lockdown.'
Project Objectives	○ Create a flexible workspace that can adapt to changing business needs and health and safety requirements over the next twelve months of flux. ○ Keep our employees, and their families safe from a virus picked up at work. ○ Provide sufficient workspaces to accommodate new

	physical distancing policies (that are still in progress)
	o Improve environmental factors such as airflow, sanitation, hygiene for employees.
	o Ensure that employees who continue to work remotely are appropriately equipped to perform their work. This includes reasonable accommodation of their furniture needs.
	o Rationalise office space where appropriate to save costs.
	o Reduce litigation risk if employees or their families take ill.
	o Assure continuity of core business functions during the move.
	o Secure hygienic workspaces.
	o Employees are located in workspaces that promote effectiveness and comply with physical distancing guidance and organisation policy.

	○ Cost efficiency in consolidation and the mixed workplace model.
Goals Be Specific, Measurable, Aligned to objectives, Realistic, Time-boxed.	○ Produce an integrated site solution plan, including facilities, buildings, furniture, equipment, OHS, and OCM by xx/xx/20 ○ Prepare the Executive Floor for occupation on xx/xx/20 ○ Complete Executive transition by xx/xx/20 ○ Complete refit of Head Office for occupation by agreed employees on xx/xx/20 ○ Complete equipping of agreed remote employees with IT, furniture, connectivity, training by xx/xx/20 ○ Complete Change Management Activities on xx/xx/20 ○ Provide Employee Engagement Survey results two months after OCM Activities.
Scope In / Out	**Phase 1 Transition** – MVP (Minimum Viable Product)

Be very clear on priority areas that are also least likely to change.	In: The following teams are in Scope: ABC, def Out: The following groups, departments, contractors are out of Scope: GHI, JKL. **Phase 2 Transition** In: The following departments are in Scope for Phase 2: MNO, PQR Out: Those not explicitly mentioned are out of the scope of this project.
Constraints What are the boundaries within which you must plan and manage?	**Schedule**: This has to be complete by xx/xx/2020 **Cost**: The cost cannot exceed $nnn **Dependencies**: You cannot perform the move over month-end or quarter-end/start. The equipment lead time may impact the critical path.
Assumptions	What have you assumed when making the above decisions? What assumptions do you have most/least confidence in, and how can I confirm those with the highest

	impact? Lowest confidence and Highest-Impact belong on the RAIDAR.
Key stakeholders	CEO, COO, CFO, CHRO, Directors, Chairman, Department Heads, Regulators, Unions, Community
Critical people for the project manager	Sponsor, Owner, OHS, Facilities Manager, Services Manager, CHRO, CFO, IT Manager, Project Management Office (PMO) if you have one.

Defining the project Deliverable or Product

It is preferable to have further detail on the required outcome of the project to have commitment and clarity in communication. This Deliverable Definition can provide the framework that drives completeness of outputs of BTF.

Figure 7 - Project Deliverable / Product example

Project Name	Back to the Future 2020
Purpose	o Create a flexible workspace that can adapt to changing business needs and health and safety requirements over the next twelve months of flux. o Provide sufficient workspaces to accommodate new physical distancing policies (that are still in progress) o Improve environmental factors such as airflow, sanitation, hygiene for employees. o Ensure that employees who continue to work remotely are appropriately equipped to perform their work. This includes reasonable

	<ul><li>accommodation of their furniture needs.</li><li>Rationalise office space where appropriate to save costs.</li><li>Cost efficiency in consolidation and the mixed workplace model.</li></ul>
Main Deliverables	<ul><li>Deliver an integrated site solution plan, including facilities, buildings, furniture, equipment, OHS, and OCM.</li><li>Complete a refit of Head Office for occupation by the agreed employees.</li><li>Complete the equipping of agreed remote employees with IT, furniture, connectivity, and training.</li><li>Complete Change Management Activities.</li><li>Post-project Employee Engagement Survey</li><li>And….</li></ul>
Inputs	<ul><li>Organisation charts</li><li>IT Inventories</li><li>Floor Plans</li><li>OHS Policies</li></ul>

	o Government COVID-19 guidance o PMO Standards and Templates o Project Definition o Facilities financial reports o And….
Skills Required	o IT Application, Collaboration, Authorisations o Procurement o Networking and Telephony o Facilities and Services o Construction and Design o PMO o Organisational Change o HR
Quality Management	Quality standards need to be defined for the different delivery functions as listed in the skills areas above.
Acceptance Criteria	o The integrated site solution plan, including facilities, buildings, furniture, equipment, OHS, and OCM o Signoff by each relevant function Executive of their project responsibilities.

	o The agreed on-site employees are fully equipped and working in an environment that meets the minimum government and OHS requirements, as well as Corporate requirements that may exceed those. o The agreed remote employees are fully equipped with IT, furniture, connectivity, and relevant enablement. o Employment contracts of all remote employees are amended for insurance and tax. o Provide Employee Engagement Survey results two months after OCM Activities.
Project Level Quality Tolerances	Are there any parameters for acceptable deviations on costs or duration? Are there any sub-projects that may be incomplete, but the overall Project Deliverable be signed off?

	(and the sub-project become a separate project?)
Acceptance Method	A Completion Report including Lessons Learned will be provided to the Steering Committee five business days before the SteerCo in month XXX/20. A Presentation will be made at the SteerCo for ratification. Comments or Changes will be clarified and adopted into the final document as appropriate. Changes might become additional work before Acceptance or Acceptance are conditional, or Changes become a separate Project.
Acceptance Responsibilities	The Steering Committee Chair (usually the Sponsor) will Accept when there is majority consensus.

9. PLANNING THE RE-LOCATION

Project Approach

The project approach defines the approach that will be taken in managing and delivering the project. This is a choice between Waterfall and Agile or a hybrid of the two. You might document some other 'approaches' or principles here that relate to decisions to be made. This avoids them being forgotten or listed as assumptions.

The Waterfall approach to defining, planning, scheduling and managing a project is the traditional model. In it, you first tie down all the requirements, agreeing on the parameters of scope, budget, deliverable/product, and time constraints. Having signed off on the needs and limitations, you identify the project phases, which include the sequence of Design, Build, Test, Deploy. Whether you have that sequence for the whole project or break the project into stages (or sprints) with precise products defined at the beginning, you are still in the Waterfall approach.

The Agile approach is different from Waterfall in the way that it iterates in sprints without the full picture of the budget, time, sequence, overall product at the beginning. This is not to imply a lack of control, but to make a broad comparison. As you can imagine, Waterfall is best for building a bridge, and Agile is excellent for nimble software development projects – and vaccine development at the moment I expect!

The problem is the confusion that can arise when some of your stakeholders say they want the project to be 'agile'. The word is often misused in a project context when they actually mean 'responsive', 'flexible', 'changeable without burdensome controls'. Make sure you are talking the same language. This project MUST be Waterfall AND 'agile' if they mean the above.

Having an 'agile' Waterfall project is possible with a robust management system that can fast-track valid change requests. Relocating offices so that they are fully functional on Day One does not allow for different teams to change what they are working on without integrating their decisions. That would be the wrong kind of 'agile'. The structure enables controlled change – How responsive your change process is depends on the organisation.

Figure 8 – Further Project 'Approach' examples

Use of Consultants	Procurement will source external consultants for the OHS and the Organisational Change projects. The consultants will report to the HR Lead. We have adequate skills and capacity in Communications, Facilities, HR and Operations.
Buy vs Lease	Any new furniture will be purchased as we expect the numbers to be low. We will re-use most furniture.

	Air conditioning units will be leased with a full-Service Level Agreement on air purity levels and maintenance.
Services	We will continue to use service providers for security and cleaning. Where additional security is required during construction, the PM is authorised to arrange directly with the provider.
Accelerators	The PM can obtain historical documents on office Re-locations from Facilities. Quality of documentation is unknown.
On-site / Remote Model	The project must propose a solution for the organisation regarding the departments or functions that MUST be on-site. It must indicate those that are PREFERRED to be on-site and those that MAY work remotely if they wish. The solution will show those that MUST work remotely.

Project Management Organisation Structure

This hierarchy represents <u>the Project Management Team</u> and not the Project Team. It shows the Roles involved in providing direction and delivery management. You will develop a structure for your own project management organisation.

Figure 9 - An example of a Project Management Team structure

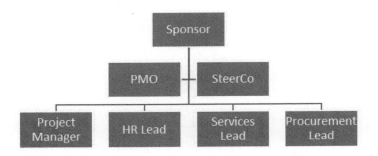

Having a comprehensive PM Organisation Structure with named actors enables you to build a management-level RACI. A RACI is explained next.

Responsible, Accountable, Consult, Inform (RACI)

The RACI is a powerful tool in holding your Teams and Stakeholders to account. Many people have many ideas, so long as they think someone else will follow through on them. It is when you say you want to assign Responsibility and Accountability; you get clarity on how important the suggestion is to the project. The same is true for anything you put into the RAIDAR. If people say to put a team, department, or distribution list as the task Owner, you refuse. Individuals are responsible and accountable – you cannot phone a group and ask a question. You cannot email a distribution list unless you KNOW it is monitored by competent people.

Figure 10 - Responsible, Accountable, Consult, Inform with examples

Product	R	A	C	I	Comments
Electrical complete	Electrician	Services Manager	Regulator	Services, PM, Regulator	Must have regulator signoff
Plumbing complete					Must have regulator signoff
Building 1 Complete	Services Manager	Site Engineer	Regulators, Suppliers	Procurement, SteerCo, Stakeholders, Regulators	Must have regulator signoff
Project Complete	Project Mgr.	Sponsor	PMO	Stakeholders	Must have Sponsor signoff

R: Responsible for delivering the Product
A: Accountable for the Product. Delegated the task to Responsible person
C: Can / Should be Consulted for guidance or approval as appropriate
I: Must be kept Informed of status.

Note: 'R' and 'A' should be only one name. It can be a title if that position is held by only one person. You need to hold individuals responsible and accountable for delivery. If you have two or more names in the R or A, your problems have just started. The lower the task in the PBS / WBS the more likely you have the name of a person.

What made the Office-to-Remote move straightforward?

In a Crisis / Chaos situation, the Objectives, Goals and Charter were the same things. These were not written down in many cases, as they were implicit and not explicit. Most managers knew enough about their areas of responsibility to understand what needed to be done urgently.

The employees did not have to be convinced of the need to move to remote working. Each employee owned their move. Changes to the home environment were the responsibility of the employee.

The objectives and goals of the move could be stated as below.

"Enable any staff who can work from home with the necessary to maintain continuity of delivery wherever possible. The enablement must allow them to be productive from the beginning of Lockdown. We are not sure when Lockdown will start, and we do not know how long it will be. Arrangements must cater for extended Lockdown but not be permanent."

The team started working from home as usual within a couple of days. They made a lot of changes in their life and work concurrently. What makes the Re-location back to the office complex?

Figure 11 - The Office-to-Remote actions are highlighted

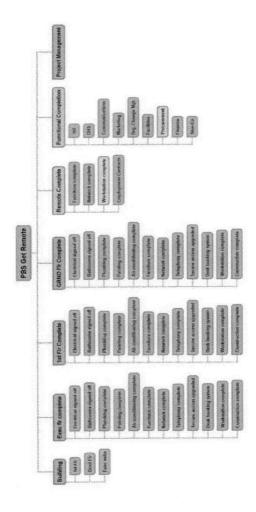

What makes the Remote-to-Office move complex?

The Relo is a Complex Project because there are so many external and internal influences. You know what is usually required to run your business, like the furnishing, facilities, parking, workstations, location of departments. But you do not see how they will be allocated and costed.

The Objective is to return to whatever 'Normal' will look like. But 'Normal' is now 'Unknown'- it is Back to the (unknowable) Future. You do not know how the business model might have changed, what new policies will be in place. You do not know what the HR policy could be towards remote work, what kind of equipment is required for each permanently remote worker.

Is the following a reasonable Objective statement? Is it enough for a project manager to run with?

"Return the appropriate staff to the campus but make provision for fewer employees. Expect to implement social distancing measures to meet yet-to-be-published government guidelines and Occupational Health. Enable agreed remote workers with all equipment needed, when that list is agreed. We are not sure when Lockdown will end. Arrangements must cater for a possible move of offices."

Figure 12 - Remote-to-Office scope example

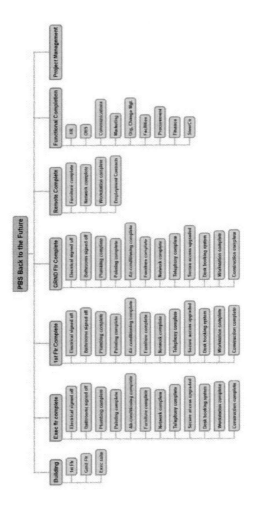

What don't we know?

- How will team dynamics change if we move to a 'hybrid' of Onsite, Remote Hub, Co-Working, and Home-Office?
- What tools, processes, and management system best suits each team?
- What will the post-lockdown office layout be?
- What is the future public transport approach?
- What rules will apply to vehicles and commuting?
- What will be compulsory, recommended, and unrestricted?
- What will the Unions want?
- What will Occupational Health require?
- What if there is a further lockdown?
- The Impact of COVID on the business:
    - Growth plans
    - Redundancy plans
    - Shortened work weeks
    - Increase in contractors during uncertainty

Scheduling Product Completion

If I ask you how long it will take to provide the Product 'Connectivity Upgraded', you will give me a high-level estimate based on experience.

If I say, I want the Product 'Connectivity Upgraded' in Stage 2 which is two weeks duration you might accept that. But if you break it down into logical steps and the period of an upgrade of domestic broadband, you know the lead time of broadband changes is usually a month. Therefore, you would arrive at something like six weeks elapsed time, even though the actual work is not 30 person-days of work. Consequently, I can accurately forecast the duration and counter the two-week request.

The Product Breakdown Structure (PBS)

You should now have at least 80% of the information you need to start planning the work.

You know the final Product required of the project, and you must break the Project Product into multiple Stage Products. Stage Products form work packages that can be allocated to teams and individuals.

For example, a Stage Product might be the 1st Floor of a building ready for staff. This is not a statement of activity but of an end-result. It is the Deliverable or Product of that Stage or Stages.

You could break the 1st Floor Product into several functional products that must be complete, for example:

- Sanitation
- Security
- Construction
- Furniture
- Networks

The 1st Floor is only ready for staff when these Products are provided. This approach highlights outcomes versus activity:

- Will the Product be ready on time?
- Will the Product provide the needed benefits?

Product Breakdown Structure Level 2 Example
Ground Floor Complete

- Electrical signed off
- Bathrooms signed off
- Plumbing complete
- Painting complete
- Air-conditioning complete
- Furniture complete
- Network complete
- Telephony complete
- Secure access upgraded
- Desk booking system
- Workstation complete
- Construction completes

Remote Complete

- Furniture complete
- Network complete
- Workstation complete
- Employment Contracts

Functional Completion

- HR
- OHS
- Communications
- Marketing
- Org, Change Mgt.
- Facilities
- Procurement
- Finance
- SteerCo
- Project Management

Figure 13 - Example PBS for a Workplace Re-location

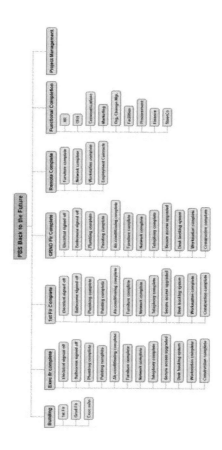

Create the Work Breakdown Structure (WBS)

You unpack the PBS to a Work Breakdown Structure as an output of Scope Management. It defines the high level ' scope of work' – the logical grouping of work at which you could assign responsibilities and do further estimating and planning.

The below WBS indicates some of the logical 'Level 3' groupings you might follow for the Relo (note: this is not a template for office Re-location, but illustrative). Below that is a 'Level 3' expansion of some of the Level 2.

Upgrade Remote workstations

- Upgrade desk/chair
- Upgrade connectivity
- Assess the current remote environment
- Investigate group rate from vendors
- Negotiate vendor contracts
- Aquire
- Upgrade workstations
- Amend Employment Contracts

Functional Completion

- HR
- OHS
- Communications
    - o Develop internal comms strategy with Org. Change Mgt.
    - o Develop external comms strategy with stakeholders
- Marketing

- o Develop media for internal change
- o Develop internal and external marketing of the changes
- o Design / procure giveaways
- Org. Change Mgt.
  - o Develop an internal communications strategy with Communications
  - o Arrange enablement sessions for hybrid organisational wow
  - o Arrange incentives for change champions
- Finance
- Project Management
  - o Project Manager
  - o Sponsor
  - o Team Managers
  - o SteerCo
- Upgrade First Flr
  - o Upgrade Electricals
  - o Refit Bathrooms
    - ▪ Define requirements
    - ▪ Design bathrooms
    - ▪ Support plumber
    - ▪ Procure fittings
- Upgrade Plumbing
  - o Review designs
  - o Determine/procure piping etc
  - o Consult Construction
  - o Perform work
- Refresh Workstations
- Re-configure Physical Space

Figure 14 - WBS Level 3 Example

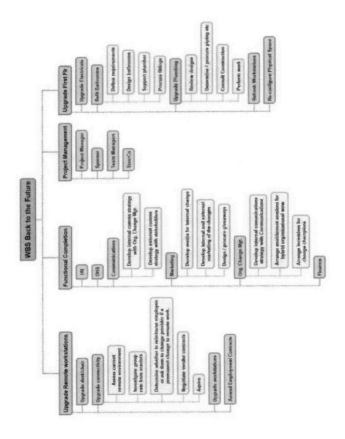

Some Information Technology WBS task examples to consider:

IT is critical to any office changes, and you cannot afford to make mistakes. Some of these tasks are more applicable to total office relocations; however, you can adapt or adopt as appropriate[3]

- Review floor plan and schedule buildout work as needed

- Identify locations for workstations, servers, printers and other hardware

- Schedule cabling and workstation assembly

- If relocating, evaluate the phone system and determine if an upgrade is warranted

- Define telecom equipment needs and location

- Schedule move date(s)

- Line up IT and moving resources

- Complete buildout work if needed

- Set up or modify network for new printers, workstations and other hardware

- Complete cabling

- Test printers

- Install workstations and furniture

---

[3] List adapted from www.rippleit.com 11/6/20

- Upgrade phone software as needed

- Install and test new workstations, phones, VOIP, VPN, security software, printers and other hardware

Evaluate your equipment. [4]

- Inventory all equipment to determine whether it still meets your needs and will be suitable in the new location.

- List any equipment that needs upgrading or replacing and order any necessary equipment.

- Return any leased IT and phone equipment that is no longer needed.

- Properly dispose of old or broken equipment.

- Evaluate server room requirements.

Assess your communications requirements.

- How many phone lines?

- For cabling, how many Cat 5 cables? Similarly, how many Cat 6 cables?

- Do I know how many power outlets there are?

- Do I know how many power outlets there are?

Prepare your site visit checklist.

- Review the configuration plan of the new office with your IT provider.

- Ensure the ideal locations for workstations, power jacks, and network cabling points are found.

---

[4] List adapted from www.switchfast.com 11/6/20

- Decide the prime location(s) for printers, scanners, routers, etc.

- Confirm whether the minimum requirements for the server room will be met (electrical, cooling, dimensions, and security).

Consider your telecommunication options.

- Review the line capacity to determine whether you need to order new phone lines.

- Set up call forwarding if you're changing your phone number.

- Establish and order the type of internet access required for the new location.

- Consider what kind of phone system is best for the new office (VoIP, PBX, etc.).

Protect your data.

- Make several backup copies of all company data systems, including firewalls and servers, store copies where they will not be affected by the move.

- Ensure full recovery is possible so that, if something does go wrong, you'll still be able to access all your company's essential data.

Prepare for Move Day.

- Transport copies of your data backup to the new location separate from the primary system and each other.

- Verify all wiring and data cables are labelled correctly and to which piece of equipment it belongs.

- Compile a contact list of everyone involved in the move.

- If needed, assist with the disconnection of infrastructure at the old office and instruct staff on how to shut down all equipment properly before leaving on the final day before the move.

Test your new office's network.

- Verify all cabling, equipment, and phones are in the right place.

- Check all individual telephone numbers and their locations.

- Test to see whether the call forwarding from the old number is working and being forwarded to the correct phone.

- Test all features of the phone system.

- Start all servers and test network capability and data migration.

- Check incoming and outgoing emails.

- Check website, intranet, and extranet.

- Test each network connection.

The lower the level of work you take, the easier to estimate. There is a trade-off on detail vs value of the effort to plan at this level though.

Figure 15 - Example of building a schedule with Level 3

Seq	Activity	Estimated duration (business days)	Estimated Start	Dependency	
1	Assess current remote environments.	2	1 June		
2	Investigate group rate from vendors.	2	3 June	1	
3	Compare the cost of a contract vs cost of reimbursement.	1	5 June	2	
4	Negotiate vendor agreement.	4	8 June	3	

Seq	Activity	Estimated duration (business days)	Estimated Start	Dependency	
5	Upgrade broadband.	20	12 June	4	Average lead time. Different lead times in different suburbs. The risk to the deadline.
6	Signoff Broadband	0	4 July	5	
	Total	**6 Weeks**			

Seq	Activity	Estimated duration (business days)	Estimated Start	Dependency	
		duration			

Building the project schedule

Project schedule management is all the activities and processes required to estimate the activities that need to be performed. It is determining the task durations and the resources that could be necessary for them. It involves identifying the lower levels of work breakdown structure as we have seen under project scope management. It would include dependencies between the different work activities as well as any resource contention that you might have. Resource contention is for people but also for specialised equipment you might have or lead times from suppliers.

Schedule Management contains processes such as defining the schedule management process, identifying the activities, and estimating activity durations. You can see that some of these happen in the start-up phase as well as in the execution phase. You are always learning during the project execution. Whether work is taking longer than expected, or the delivery of equipment is delayed, you might find that you need to do re-estimating and adjust your schedule.

I have a friend who was equipping of a large hotel with wrought-iron balconies. The project manager had every supplier on an incentivised performance contract, and therefore there was little coordination between them. Each supplier was intent on completing the work as soon as possible. The people installing the wrought-iron balcony railings were welding when the carpets one metre away had already been laid. Curtains were already hanging in the window opening.

So, although some of your suppliers may be ready ahead of time, you will probably not have anywhere to store their deliveries. Delays on the critical path could then delay the installation of the furniture which is being stored by the vendor. If they do not have the people available to transport and install, then your project is further impacted.

When building your estimates and dependencies, you need to include contingency time as part of risk management. You will find it helpful to have delivery milestones in the case of the office-to-office move, and potentially in the Relo move.

With the COVID-19 move, there was not much time if any available for building a schedule. The schedule was a move as soon as possible. The urgency was to re-use the equipment which was already in use, as well as workstations and chairs. There was no time to order new equipment or to wait for the IT department to transport and install your workstation at home.

When we look at the Relo project, we again have a problem determining a schedule. We may not know the actual times at which we have to make moves because strategic considerations will drive that. We must plan on what we know. It may seem strange that we can plan on what we don't know. If we know what we don't know, we can plan up to that point and then be hyper-alert to when those outstanding questions are answered.

Whereas the move to remote working was driven by line management and team leaders. I hope that the movement back to the unknown will be managed centrally – and that might be you. There are pros and cons to having this preparation done centrally. Unless the central function is consulting widely enough with line management, trouble lurks around the next corner. An example would be the ordering of screens to go between desks as part of the government workplace guidelines.

If you order screens based on the old normal, you will almost definitely have more than you need and probably have to wait longer for them. You could unnecessarily spend a lot of effort rearranging office allocations within a building. You could use budget preparing the old offices instead of on equipping the permanent remote workers. Or, you might be equipping people for remote work who will inevitably be relocated on-site.

The schedule in a Gantt Chart

The amount of detail needed in your project depends on the scope, dependencies, risks, departments, geographies, and locations, amongst other factors. The figure below is known as a Gantt Chart and shows tasks or work packages (but is not an actual Relo guide!). The more complexity, the higher the risk, and therefore the greater the need for control. This template exists in Microsoft Excel, but if the complexity and risk warrant it, you might choose an off-the-shelf project planning and tracking tool.

Figure 16 - Illustrative Scheduling - Conceptual only

Office to Office Project Planner

Select a period to highlight at right. A legend describing the charting follows.

ACTIVITY	PLAN START	PLAN DURATION	ACTUAL START	ACTUAL DURATION	PERCENT COMPLETE	PERIODS 1 2 3 4 5 6 7 8 9 10 11 12 13 14 15 16 17 18
Create Project Charter	1	1	1	1	100%	
Assign Project Manager	1	1	1	1	100%	
Confirm Requirements	2	1	2	1	100%	
Confirm Scope	2	1	2	1	100%	
Create Project Management Plan	3	2	2		85%	
Confirm Stakeholders	3	1	2		85%	
Create Communications Plan	3	1	2		50%	
Create Project Schedule	4	1			0%	
Create Budget	4	1			0%	
Create Resource Plan	4	1			0%	
Create Procurement Plan	4	2			0%	
Create Work Breakdown Structure	4	2			0%	
Assign IT Team Leader	9	1			0%	
Assign Facilities Team Leader	9	1				
Assign HR Representative	9	1			0%	
Assign Marketing / Communications Lead	9	1				
Create New Office Requirements Definition	3	2	3		80%	
Assign Procurement Team Lead	3	1			0%	
Assign Finance Representative	3	1			0%	
Assign Property Agencies	5	2			0%	
Tender for Office Design Co.	5	1			0%	
Tender for Relocation Co.	5	1			0%	
Tender for Construction and Repairs Co.	5	1			0%	
Review Properties	6	2			0%	
Sign Contracts	8	2			0%	
Approve Interior Designs	10	1			0%	
Approve Construction Plans	10	1			0%	
Phase 1 Milestone	12	0			0%	
Perform Construction and Interior Décor	14	4			0%	
Install Furniture	18	4			0%	
Install Networking	18	2			0%	
Install Workstations	20	1			0%	
Phase 2 Milestone	22	0			0%	

Period Highlight: 1   Plan Duration   Actual Start   % Complete

10.   MANAGE THE PROJECT

Managing the project requires you to pull together the information regarding progress as measured, including but not limited to delays, risks, issues, changes, resources, costs, dependencies, and conflicts.

Consider the processes in project scope management. These processes are there to define the scope and work involved in the project, having clarified the requirements. With the range of work assigned, you then have your scope management plan against which you monitor the risk of scope creep. Having a scope management plan, a resource management plan, a cost management plan, a procurement management plan, and the Risk Register to mitigate the risks that are common to most projects.

In the start-up, initiation, and planning phases your management system will be developed. Your system includes the following reporting cycles and meetings as appropriate for the importance and complexity of your project.

Some meetings you may have in your management system:

- Steering Committee / Project Board
- Weekly Team Manager Project Status
- Weekly Team Manager 1-1
- Weekly Risk Review
- Weekly Sponsor check-in
- Stage End / Start

- Quality Management Review
- Stakeholder Review

Reports you may produce include:

- Steering Committee / Project Board
- Weekly Status and Health
- Financial Report
- Milestone Report
- Testing
- Stage End
- Resource Requirements
- Vendor Management

A note on meetings

Be aware that every meeting takes productive time out of the project. It is not uncommon to have members of the delivery teams spending twenty per cent of their week in meetings. If my group of eight attends a weekly meeting together, they lose one hour of coding and testing each – and I lose a full person-day of productive time. If they attend a one-hour team meeting with the customer, there go another 8 hours. Then they have a one to one with the architect, a demo to the customer, and they have lost four coding hours each (and the Architect even more).

As the Project Manager on the Relo project, you could have eight Team Managers and the risk that you are all in too many meetings. Sure, it is necessary to have cross-functional meetings where responsibilities overlap. Still, then it is up to you to prepare well so that the meeting is only as long as it has to be.

My recommendation is to regularly review the purpose of, and participants in, every meeting. The name of the meeting and the actual reason may have long since been different things. Not all attendees are participants, so why are they there?

- What is the goal of the meeting? How specific is it?
- How often does the meeting not result in the outcome? Who or what is missing when that happens?
- Who is in the meeting because they always have been, but may not be needed now? Who is better

served by being on an email cc, instead of in the room for information only?

- Do you hold meetings when the decision-maker is regularly absent? This can mean they are too busy or disinterested – both are bad signs. Other essential participants may take similar liberties from her example.
- Who regularly sends an uninformed delegate? If this is a frequent challenge, ask the intended participant to nominate and empower their delegate as the permanent representative.
- Who is always on his laptop during the meeting? This can mean they have no good reason to be there.

Tracking the project health

Let's remind ourselves of the six key indicators making a dashboard for your project health. This is the same template as previously shown, with more questions you can ask yourself.

Figure 17 - 6 Key Indicators of Project Health

6 Keys	RAG	Comments
Stakeholder Commitment	G	See the tables that follow.
Scope Management	G	
Business Benefits	G	
Risk Management	G	
Team Performance	G	
Work and Schedule	G	

Figure 18 - Stakeholder health indicators

Stakeholders are Committed	Stakeholders are known.
	The right Sponsor is appropriately engaged.
	Regular Steering Committee meetings held and documented.
	All appropriate stakeholder groups are represented and effectively involved.
	Actions or decisions are taken in a timely fashion.
	All stakeholders are satisfied.
	Their interests and influence are identified.
	Their change over time is monitored.
	Stakeholders are available.

Figure 19 - Business Benefits Realisation indicators

Business Benefits Realised	The business case is clearly and convincingly articulated.
	Benefits are measurable and achievable.
	The solution will appropriately support the desired outcomes.
	Sponsor has confidence in the delivery organisation.

Figure 20 - Work and Schedule indicators

Work and Schedule are Predictable		Interim and final milestones are clearly defined and agreed.
	Predictable	Project is using an appropriate and realistic approach.
		Work-stream plans are correctly integrated and used to manage delivery.
		There is an appropriate basis for confidence in the accuracy of progress reports and estimates to completion.
		Deadlines are being met.
		Actuals are being tracked against the plan.

Figure 21 - Team performance indicators

Team	The project is fully staffed with appropriately skilled resources.
	The team is motivated.
	The working environment supports productive and effective teamwork.
	There is constant communication between the PM and the Team.
	The work is being achieved with regular working hours.
	There is a continuity of critical people.

Figure 22 - Scope health indicators

Scope	Delivery commitments are feasible, compared to other similar projects
	Project boundaries are appropriately defined in a signed, written agreement
	Roles and responsibilities are clearly agreed
	Proposed/agreed changes are appropriately reflected in costs, schedules and responsibilities

Figure 23 - Risk health indicators

Risks	Risks have been appropriately identified, with mitigating actions.
	The risk management plan is being used to appropriately control risks.
	Quality of work products is appropriate.
	The Team is notified of the increased chance of a risk event.

Project progress report examples

Progress reporting is another aspect that should fit the needs of the stakeholders and the complexity. If your Team Managers are using the same template as each other and you, communication is enhanced. It is then so much easier for you to consolidate the information into a Project level report, and ultimately into a SteerCo report.

Figure 24 - Team Reporting Template

Reporting period

From		To	

Reporter:

Key Accomplishments

Project	Back to the Future
Date of report	
Workstream	
Key Risks, Issues, Changes	

Owner	Due

Activities last period

Activity	Due	Status

Activities next period

Activity	Due	Status

7 Keys	RAG	Comments
Stakeholder Commitment		
Scope Management		
Business Benefits		
Risk Management		
Team Performance		
Work and Schedule		
Delivery Organisation Benefits		

Figure 25 - Project Manager Report Template

Project				
Date of report				
Workstream	All Workstreams			
Key Risks,	Description	Owner	Due	

Key actions			
Workstream		Due	RAG

Reporting period		
From	To	
Reporter:		
Key Accomplishments		

Progress Summary		RAG
Workstream		
Facilities		
IT		
Construction		
Procurement		
Human Resources		
OHS		
Org. Change		
Marketing		
Finance		
Communications		
Utilities		
Legal		

Action Log

The most common problem I encounter when sent to a troubled project is the lack of a simple Action Log. We all tend to over-engineer our management system if working with an external customer or trying to please a demanding stakeholder. My advice is to start small if the complexity is unclear.

Don't build a system to manage the construction of the Golden Gate Bridge when you are making a pedestrian walkway in the botanical gardens. Delays, Disputes and Disasters are often calmed by the presence of one view of project status. Take your Risks, Issues, Changes and Dependencies and make sure they always have relevant actions in the Action Log. Do not try to manage Actions in several places – just cross-reference the Action to the RIDs.

Your stakeholders would far rather know exactly what is outstanding and who is responsible for moving forward. They are less interested in proving who was responsible for getting where you are! (That discussion can come later. For now, remember the RACI on the escalated Issues and Actions.)

Figure 26 - Action Log Example

Action ID	Xref	Status	Action	Raised	Assigned	Due	Started	Complete	Priority	Source	Product	Function	Type	Owner
A01	R01	Open	Sanitising gel and wipes at the place of use.	30-May	01-Jun	05-Jun			High		John	Electricity	Project Mg	Peter
A02	R02	Assigned	Review frequency of disinfection.	30-May							Peter	Water	Facilities	Paul
A03	R03	Active	Install touchless security, automated doors, sanitiser and wipes at point of entry.	30-May							Jane	Sanitation	HR	Mary
A04	R04	Late	Spacing and perspective of workstations, screens.	30-May							Mary	Construction	Procureme	Jane
A05	R05	Escalated	Put access control on doors, review frequency of cleaning, sanitiser at points of entry. Push doors open from inside.	30-May							TBC	Security	Constructii	Same
A06	R06	On Hold	Restrict access of visitors, create 'safe spaces' for visitor interaction.	30-May								Furniture	Org. Chang	Ralph
A07	R07	Closed	Provide some kind of spray or device with disinfectat properties that will not damage the packaging or contents.	30-May								Workstations	Utilities	Deshan
A08	R08		Create one-way passages with some room for passing, but only one-way.	30-May								Networks	Services	ishmail
A09	R09		To be reviewed by needs.	30-May								Above are list examples			
A10	R10		Sanitising gel and wipes at the place of use, and cleaning frequency increased. Provide technology that does not need direct contact with whiteboards or pens (and/or make the pens single-use disposable).	30-May											

Issue and Change Register

Issues and Changes are also useful to have in a Workbook so that the cross-referencing of Actions to Risks, Issues and Changes are only a tab away.

Issues can arise from several sources, but in all cases, they should be headed off when only a 'problem'. A 'problem' is a deviation or anomaly or point of contention that is resolved within the relevant team or team managers. The aim is to address it before it becomes an Exception that cannot be resolved within the project manager's scope of authority and influence. When it cannot be resolved within the team, it becomes an Issue, and Issues affect the RAG of a task or project.

Changes can arise during development, demonstrations, defects and delivery. Not all changes need to be the subject of investigation and analysis if it is simple to estimate the work required, and the impact on resources is minimal. However, put them in the Register because they can come back and bite you if many small improvements or amendments impact the costs, schedule and product quality.

Reactive Changes in the Project Environment are the most significant Project Risks you should anticipate in the COVID-19 Relo. If you break your project into small enough 'Stages' and are planning in detail only a certain way ahead, you can be more responsive to change. Critical is to have a robust management system.

Figure 27 - Issue / Change Register Example

Issue IDX ref / Change short descrip	Issue / Change Long description	Date Raised	Source	Category	Function	Type	Date Assigned	Analysed	Plan	Impact Cost	Duration	Effort	Quality	Benefits	Owner
Issd1	Expand our scope to incl	Issue is that we get no extra budget		John	Scope	Project Mgt	Issue				200	10	5			
Ch01	Include another meeting; increases costs for screens and access control		Peter	Time	Facilities	Change				300	5	5			
Ch02	Exclude 5 employees	This is good news as we struggled for floor space		Jane	Cost	HR	Change				-200	0	-5			
Issd2	Delay on door	Door is coming 2 weeks late. This delays fitting access t		Mary	Quality	Procurement	Issue					14	0			
Ch03	Include 2 other dept emp	We can include in plan but need budget from that dept.		TBC	Team	Construction	Change				100	5	10			
Ch04	Plumber needs to sub-co	Has to come from contingency.			Benefits	Org. Change	Change				100	0	0			
					Utilities										
					Services										

Above are list examples

Managing your costs

Project cost management is the process of pulling together an overall budget for the project. You will be developing your cost management plan. This details how you will be managing the budget and tracking costs and reporting them to your project owner or CFO. You need to know if there is a project management office to whom you provide reports or if there is a system you must use.

It is essential to understand how costs will be allocated to the project. Has the overall budget of the project included any capital costs or start-up costs from the functional areas, or will they be charged directly? For example, any computer equipment and auxiliary equipment that has to be purchased for the move is ultimately charged back to the using department. Still, for reporting purposes are they going to use your project cost code or the cost code of the functional area or the department receiving those items. The same question applies to any transitional services.

Very often, there is no system, and when I am managing projects for clients, they will tell me to use whatever method I am accustomed to. I am not in favour of this approach because somewhere along the line, any project could be audited. I would prefer the project budget to be tracked, including my input, but with an overall cost report going to the client stakeholders. It is striking to me how many customers do not have the standard reporting and tracking mechanism even though they are very sophisticated businesses. There is a trend towards better tracking of project costs, including a customer costing their internal resources to the project. In that way, they see the total costs of the project, including resources they are allocating who might end up waiting when there are delays.

You must consider costs for all elements of the WBS. Check with the Owner or CFO whether they want to track the internal expenses for your project management. Some companies will have an internal charge-back system. For example, if you are an IT Project Manager who has been assigned the office-to-office project, your management may seek relief on their budget.

Here are some of the costs involved in an office relocation

- Lease early cancellation fee for current building if applicable
- Up-front payment on the new lease
- Repairs to old buildings (Dilapidations)
- Construction of the new office layout
- Furniture (don't forget special needs accommodation)
- Storage costs
- Moving costs
- New workplace technologies
- Disposal of old furniture and technology
- Upfront costs for new service providers
- Final costs at old premises
- Updating details across all suppliers and customers and stakeholders
- Insurance

Costs for the urgent move to remote working might be reimbursed or funded by a central contingency fund within the organisation. It is then up to the finance department to reallocate the money from somewhere else or to claim on insurance if they have that kind of cover. In most cases, the move to remote work was achieved with minimal setup cost. However, there would have been some employees who did not have their own workstations, or furniture, or adequate data on their mobile phone contracts. Not everyone has the monthly cash flow to increase their communications or home office at their expense. Even saying it will be reimbursed later might not make it easier.

The following table illustrates where costs can be expected in a typical move and a complicated move from remote to future. It assumes that the Relo is back to the existing building and not to a new one at this point.

Figure 28 - Examples of cost elements in workplace transitions

Cost Element / Impact	Office-to-Office	Office-to-Remote	Remote-to-Unknown
Lease early cancellation fee for the current building	High	No	No
Up-front payment on the new lease	High	No	No
Repairs to old buildings (Dilapidations)	Yes	No	No
Construction of the new office layout	High	No	Med.
Furniture (don't forget special needs accommodation)	High	Low	Med.
Storage costs	Med.	No	Med.
Moving costs	High	Low	Low
New workplace technologies	Med.	Low	Low
Disposal of old furniture and technology	Low	No	Low
Upfront costs for new service providers	Med.	Low	Low
Final costs at old premises	Med.	No	No
Updating details across all suppliers and customers and stakeholders	Low	No	No

Managing Product quality

Your primary measure of project product quality is the readiness and willingness of employees to move back into the workplace. The critical aspects of this were explained in the Change Management chapter.

For other products, you should adhere to the organisational quality management policies. However, you may find they have limited applicability to your move unless you are a moving company. You must learn how your organisation defines and measures quality, and expectations of continuous improvement in projects and operations. Given this, you will be better equipped to set standards for the end of the project, and for your different functional areas to deliver. This is particularly important with strategic projects such as office relocation, where you have several suppliers on whom you rely. Not only are you reliant on the quality of their product and service but also on the timeliness in meeting commitments. A supplier who misses a commitment could delay the next piece of work, which might have cost implications for you and the quality of the project.

When looking at the Re-location, you have several moving parts which require quality standards of some kind to end with a quality result meeting your Sponsor's requirement in full. You do not want to over-design or over-engineer the quality requirements, because you end up paying for the inspection and rework which is not necessary. You want a practical working fit-for-purpose defect-free environment. You want everything to be delivered on time with the correct level of skilled personnel who can then install and configure in the time committed. You do not want the supplier to finish later than planned, nor do you want them to rush the job and compromise the quality. Defects result in rework, which costs somebody more money.

Quality requirements must be written into vendor contracts regarding products, services and warranties.

Planning your project resources — teams, equipment, services, materials

This used to be called the project human resource management knowledge area. It has been acknowledged that the project manager is responsible for more than just people depending on the type of project. If you consider the Relo, some small businesses might choose to rent their own van to transport old equipment from one building to the other. Therefore, the project manager would be responsible for ensuring it is booked, hired, and available on the days needed. If the rental company provides a driver, then all is good. Still, if not, the project manager must arrange for a driver and some help for the fetching and carrying.

You can draw on a few inputs based on past projects and advice from your suppliers. Remember this knowledge area refers to the people and technologies required for the life of the project, and not after handover. The larger and the more complicated it becomes then you may need to add key members to your team.

Whether your team is part-time or full time assigned to the project, you are responsible for providing leadership and management. You ensure they deliver on their responsibilities in line with the project schedule and quality requirements. As this is an office move and not a sophisticated engineering or information technology project, most of the responsibility probably falls to you as the project manager.

Designing and Managing project communications

The instructor on my first project management course said there are three rules to project management. The first, second, and third rule is to communicate.

Do not underestimate the importance of communication and consultation as part of the change this project brings about. You are managing much more than a change in an office location.

The three main processes involved in project communications management are the **planning**, the **management**, and **monitoring** that the communications are meeting your objectives and the needs of the target audience.

The problem we have is that everybody is overloaded with information. Information is coming in emails, apps, flyers, booklets, web pages, texts, inline ads, and podcast ads. How are we supposed to break through the noise? Communications management means thinking outside of the box when communicating with some people. Project communications management includes developing a strategy that gets the right information to the right people at the right time. It is how you give confidence to your project sponsor and other stakeholders that you are in control of the project. They can, therefore, make business decisions based on your delivery timeline.

You will have two types of communication in most projects – Factual progress reporting, and Change messaging. You have communication to your senior stakeholders about financial progress and achievement of project milestones.

Other stakeholders needing only the facts are external market analysts if it has a significant impact on the way that you deliver products and services externally. If you are only transforming an internal department or function with internal users, you will not necessarily be overly concerned about external stakeholders.

11.   CLOSING THE PROJECT

When you can demonstrate the project requirements are met, you must get closure from the Steering Committee. The objective is to confirm you delivered to the charter within the tolerances. If there were changes to the scope, time, cost, or product, you need evidence of controlled change.

Now you pull together all project documentation. The documentation includes that used to define and manage the project, as well as that produced.

Project Definition documents include:
- Charter / Brief
- Project Initiation
- Project Plan
- Contracts
- Business Case

Project Management Plans for:
- Integration
- Scope
- Time
- Cost
- Procurement
- Risks
- Issues
- Resources
- Schedule

Project Control documents such as:

- Configuration control
- Product acceptances
- Change control
- Issue register
- Risk register
- Financial reports
- Project Schedule
- Knowledge Base
- Reports
  - Steering Committee / Board
  - Regulatory
  - Weekly Project Reports
  - Minutes of meetings
  - Lessons Learned

Project Products

- Architectural drawings
- Building approvals
- Compliance certificates
- Contracts
- Maintenance Agreements
- Work completion acceptances
- Union acceptance
- HSE acceptance

With the documentation in hand, you are cross-referencing to the Project Definition and Project Plan to validate the following:.

- Have we done what we said we would do?
- Have we closed off on the construction work? Is everything on the snag list complete?
- Have we finished with all of the communications around change management?
- Have we reconciled and closed the budget?
- Have we notified the regulators?
- Have we notified other bodies within the organisation who need to know that you are no longer in charge?
- Has this been handed over to the facilities or services area?

This is the point for releasing team members who have been reporting to you directly. Remember to commend top performers to their manager. This is important for their performance reviews and fosters your relationship with the employee and the manager.

So, as you enter into this closing out of the project, there are several items you want to have in a final report which will go to your steering committee for final approval. Critical in that report is a summary for the executives. Repeat the initial vision and objectives of the project. Provide them with a reminder of what the scope and goals were. You want to remind them of the criteria that were used for keeping the project on track. This also confirms that the completion criteria have been met during and at the end of the project. Document that you satisfied the quality metrics as you got to the end of each stage or phase. Confirm the quality of the deliverables both during stages and of the final product of the project.

Your closing report will detail the financials of the project. There should be no surprises here. You would have advised your steering committee of any financials moving outside of the agreed tolerances. If those tolerances were being exceeded regularly, you would have been updating the project. You would have included that in your review of the business case business benefits during the project. If the business en.vironment changes to the point that the Relo is impractical, this project could have had a premature completion (Premature completion is not always a failure.). Report how the schedule was actually managed and tracked and highlight learnings around the estimation.

You will also include documents that support the handover to the operational environment. These will be facilities, security services, cleaning, maintenance, and procurement for ongoing contracts. It is when you have a final signature from those different operational facilities that you can claim that this project is complete. You can fully release all resources close all contracts and ask to be assigned to a new project.

12.   CONCLUSION

At the beginning of the book, I said we would look at the Re-location of remote workers back to the future. From the time you picked the book up to now, several aspects of your life will have changed. Indeed, the trauma of the COVID-19 pandemic lives on, and we all seek to make sense of it. You and I, and those for whom you are organising this transition to the future world of work, are having to find our feet as we go. This is not a transformation programme that was years in the planning. This transition to the next normal, the new normal, the future way of working, did not arise in someone's mind as part of a strategy. It did not go through all of the phases of organisational change in planning and execution. Although many companies would have been considering more people working remotely, this was probably regarded as part of an overall strategy. Instead, it all happened in the most unstructured of ways. You saw natural leaders emerge. You saw people learn technologies almost immediately.

Previously we would have looked at who has the maturity and self-discipline to be trusted to work at home. Instead, we found we had to trust everybody. And the surprise is that some we would doubt have proven to be more effective when working from home. Others who we thought would be excellent remote workers may have shown themselves to be less useful from home. This is because there were so many variables involved. It's a complicated situation, and you could not have anticipated the inflight business strategy decisions that have by necessity been made.

There are many lessons to be learned during this time and project. Yours is one of the first in your company; therefore, you must document and share this new-found knowledge.

When somebody said move people back, they thought it was simple, and you may have felt similarly. On the other hand, you may have recognised the complexity and the chance to stand out from the crowd. No matter if the former or the latter, I hope that this short book has given you enough of the building blocks to rapidly start and remain in control as you progress.

My hope is that this book has provided you with a jump start and with a framework and that you might choose to look deeper into project management as a career.

Printed in Poland
by Amazon Fulfillment
Poland Sp. z o.o., Wrocław